DEVON'S
BEAUTIFUL BUILDINGS

Philip Knowling & Lee Pengelly

HALSGROVE

First published in Great Britain in 2003

Text © 2003 Philip Knowling
Images © 2003 Lee Pengelly

British Library Cataloguing-in-Publication Data
A CIP record for this title is available from the British Library

ISBN 1 84114 279 4

HALSGROVE

Halsgrove House
Lower Moor Way
Tiverton, Devon EX16 6SS
Tel: 01884 243242
Fax: 01884 243325
email: sales@halsgrove.com
website: www.halsgrove.com

Printed by D'Auria Industrie Grafiche Spa, Italy

CONTENTS

ACKNOWLEDGEMENTS

Lord Clifford
Debbie Griffiths, Dartmoor National Park Authority
Devon Historic Buildings Trust
Jenny Sanders, the Devonshire Association
John Maidment, East Devon District Council
Tony Rees, English Heritage
Mark Stobbs, Exeter City Council
Simon Hoare
Vince Hallam
Liz Knowling
Katherine Oakes, the Landmark Trust
Brian Le Messurier
Kevin Dearing, Mid Devon District Council
Catherine Marlow, Mid Devon District Council
Collette Hall, North Devon District Council
Rachel Broomfield, Historic Environment Department, Plymouth City Council.
Graham Lawrence, Teignbridge District Council
Christopher Pancheri, Torbay Council
Jill Baines, University of Exeter

PHOTOGRAPHIC LOCATIONS

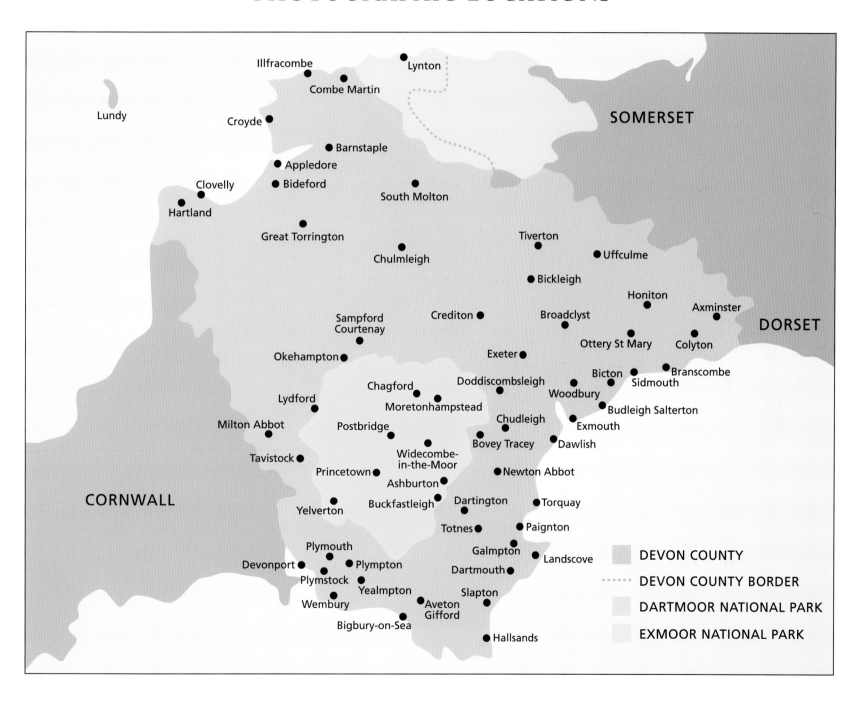

Lundy

SOMERSET

Illfracombe
Lynton
Combe Martin
Croyde
Barnstaple
Appledore
Clovelly
Bideford
South Molton
Hartland
Great Torrington
Tiverton
Chulmleigh
Uffculme
Bickleigh
Honiton
Axminster
Sampford Courtenay
Crediton
Broadclyst
DORSET
Okehampton
Exeter
Ottery St Mary
Colyton
Chagford
Doddiscombsleigh
Bicton
Branscombe
Lydford
Moretonhampstead
Woodbury
Sidmouth
Milton Abbot
Postbridge
Chudleigh
Budleigh Salterton
Exmouth
Widecombe-in-the-Moor
Bovey Tracey
Dawlish
Tavistock
Princetown
Ashburton
Newton Abbot
CORNWALL
Yelverton
Buckfastleigh
Dartington
Torquay
Totnes
Paignton
Plymouth
Galmpton
Landscove
Devonport
Plympton
Dartmouth
Plymstock
Yealmpton
Slapton
Wembury
Aveton Gifford
Bigbury-on-Sea
Hallsands

DEVON COUNTY
DEVON COUNTY BORDER
DARTMOOR NATIONAL PARK
EXMOOR NATIONAL PARK

Old cinema, the Strand, Barnstaple
A striking art deco cinema built out of bold blocks of pastel colour.

INTRODUCTION

There are far more beautiful buildings in Devon than can be gathered in one volume. This is merely a sample of what the county has to offer. We hope that our choices will find favour but also that they will stimulate discussion and perhaps challenge a few preconceptions.

Devon's building history is well recorded – Nikolas Pevsner and Bridget Cherry, W. G. Hoskins, Peter Beacham and others have seen to that. This book is not an academic treatise, but more a celebration of what has been studied.

What is a beautiful building?

What makes a building beautiful? It's not greatness – an architecturally significant building does not have to be attractive, while an ordinary cottage of no historical merit may be pretty. The appeal can be in the style, materials, setting or even the mood of the moment. Beauty is in the eye of the beholder, so any collection of this nature is by definition subjective.

Buildings are rarely beautiful in isolation – neighbouring buildings, gardens or the wider landscape complete the picture. We have tried to reflect this by showing appropriate buildings in their settings. Sometimes the appeal is in a whole street – the beauty of a row of buildings can be greater than the sum of the parts.

Detail: St Mary's church, Ottery St Mary

A fragment of a building can also be beautiful – an archway here, a window there, for instance. Moulded bricks, gargoyles, stained glass, finials and doorknobs can all make magic. The delight is in the detail.

The importance of buildings

The importance of buildings goes far beyond their perceived beauty. Buildings are, at their most basic, little more than shelter – but as styles and techniques have evolved, they have become historical documents. They mirror the state of the society in which they were built and the status of the people for whom they were built.

Buildings are one way of telling the history of people. They show how we have lived and worked, played and prayed, fought and died. Buildings also tell the story of a county. They echo the geology and (through the use of wood and thatch) the botany of the land.

Buildings reflect the industry of a county. Shipyards, mine-workings, potteries, limekilns, wind- and water-mills, factories and warehouses are the built evidence of centuries of endeavour. With these come the canals, roads, railways and bridges which are built but not (in the accepted sense) buildings.

Agriculture has likewise left us a built legacy. There are farmhouses, longhouses, ash houses, roundhouses, barns and linhays. The fading fortunes of farming have sent this legacy into decline. An old and once-proud barn that has fallen into decay is a metaphor for the state of modern agriculture.

Another aspect of our built environment is lifestyle architecture – buildings for leisure and pleasure. They include pubs, theatres, swimming baths, sports stadia, cinemas and bowling-alleys. Many of these have long histories, but the modern-day proliferation shows that we have more free time and spare money, and more ways in which to spend them both, than ever before.

Public buildings are clues to social history. People can be traced by their churches, chapels, mosques and synagogues (Plymouth has the oldest Ashkenazi temple in England, dating from 1762). Airports and railway stations, hospitals and town halls chart the progress of modernisation.

Private houses have an impact on the landscape. In the past a small number of large houses influenced the countryside with their gardens, parks and attendant estates. Today it is the large number of small houses for ordinary people that has the biggest effect.

Building materials

Historically, the buildings of any county were made out of what that county had to offer. Vernacular architecture means building with what is to hand.

To simplify a complicated geology, Devon is built largely of granite, limestone, sandstone and slate – which means that so too are its buildings. Overlying the geological foundations are the organic materials that have been used along with the stones – wood, thatch and cob (a mix of clay and straw, used wet). In addition, trade introduced materials and ideas from further afield; bricks from the Netherlands, new styles from trend-setting London, for example.

While thatch has remained in regular use, it is interesting to observe a revival of interest in cob. Today we have cob bus shelters and building companies that specialise in cob; a new cob barn has just been built at Cockington, in Torquay. It's good to see that artists and sculptors are also working with this traditional material.

The diversity of Devon

Biodiversity is an environmental buzz-word. Nature conservation recognises the value of maintaining a wide range of species, eco-systems and habitats. We should also be aware of the diversity of our built environment. That's why this book attempts to reflect the extraordinary diversity of buildings in Devon.

We have tried to represent the themes that have contributed to the character of the county. Prehistory, farming, seafaring, the military, trade, industry and the Church are included. There are big houses, little houses, ruins and curiosities. Importantly, there is a mix of ancient and modern.

Architects of Devon

Many notable architects and landscapers have worked in Devon, including August Pugin (the mausoleum at Bicton), John Nash (Luscombe Castle, Sandridge at Stoke Gabriel), Robert Adam (Saltram), William Burges (Knightshayes Court), Sir Edwin Lutyens (Castle Drogo), Capability Brown (Ugbrooke) and Humphry (or Humphrey) Repton (Luscombe, Endsleigh).

Others had limited input, including Sir John Soane, Sir John Vanbrugh (in the dockyard at Plymouth), Sir George Gilbert Scott (mainly church restorations) and Gertrude Jekyll (in the form of advice).

Oak Park House, Dawlish, nineteenth century
*A grand Victorian villa, Italianate and stuccoed,
complete with a campanile.*

While the great phases and fashions of architecture ebbed and flowed, the constant undercurrent was, of course, vernacular architecture. Simple traditions continued by anonymous local builders make up the majority of the dwellings. The most enduring symbol of Devon's vernacular is the longhouse.

If Devon has its own architect, then perhaps it is John Foulston (1772–1842). He came to Plymouth from London in 1811 after winning a competition to design public buildings. He arrived at a time of great industry and development but when Plymouth, Stonehouse and Devonport were still separate towns.

Foulston brought neoclassical style to Plymouth with his public buildings, terraces and villas. He also built Union Street to connect the settlements and introduced grid-system street plans. Sadly, much of his work has been destroyed or disfigured by war and subsequent development.

Buildings by John Foulston can still be seen in central Plymouth, while in Ker Street, Devonport, stand the remains of a remarkable group of public buildings. Completed in 1824, the set originally featured a neoclassical town hall, an Egyptian-style institution, a 'Hindoo' (Indian) chapel and a Grecian column. The chapel has gone, the grand classical terraces surrounding the group have been razed and the remaining buildings are in poor shape. It's a sad state of affairs for public architecture of such imagination.

Foulston also carried out alterations at Saltram House (1818, 1820), built an uncharacteristic cottage ornée, complete with rustic tree-trunk pillars, in Torquay (Woodbine Cottage, 1823, since demolished), and worked in Tavistock (the restoration of Tavistock Abbey gatehouse for the Duke of Bedford was a rare excursion into the Gothic style).

One or two others should be remembered. Around the turn of the nineteenth century Sir Thomas Tyrwhitt was putting great energies into taming Dartmoor with agriculture and architecture. Born in 1762, he was educated at Eton and Oxford and became a public servant in the household of the Prince of Wales.

Tyrwhitt recognised the commercial benefits of conquering and exploiting Dartmoor. He caused roads and the railway to be constructed, established the gaol for prisoners of the Napoleonic Wars (seeing the men as a workforce to further his own business aims) and founded Princetown.

During the late-nineteenth and early-twentieth centuries W.D. Caroë made his mark on Devon, mainly through the design or restoration of churches. He worked on restorations such as St Winfred's, Branscombe (1911), and contributed decorative work, for instance, at Crediton.

The church of St David, on St David's Hill, Exeter (1900), is said to be Caroë's finest building. He also designed St Sabinus at Woolacombe (1910), St Gabriel, Peverell, Plymouth (1910 onwards) and St Francis, Sidmouth (1929).

Farms

Despite its towns and cities and the spread of modern housing, Devon is still a rural county. The landscape is agricultural and generally medieval in origin, with cottages, farmsteads and manor houses scattered across the countryside.

A typical Devon farmstead might consist of a house and ranges of outbuildings (of thatch and stone or cob) joined to enclose a yard. Often on

Cob buildings, Chulmleigh

the side of a hill, with high walls and small windows, they present a defensive aspect. Some of these fortress farms have hardly changed their appearance in 500 years.

What has been left out

There are different reasons why buildings have been omitted from this collection. Firstly, it was of course impossible to include every building in Devon that might be thought beautiful.

Secondly, many beautiful buildings were unavailable to us. Some were off limits because their owners preferred them not to be photographed; naturally we respected their wishes. And I should add here that inclusion in this book is not an invitation to visit. Many properties are (happily) open to the public, but others are not.

Some buildings were ruled out because they were simply impossible to photograph well. Sadly, a good number had to be excluded due to decay. Many of the buildings that should be among Devon's most beautiful are – for one reason or another – crumbling wrecks and derelict shells.

This is a state of affairs which local authorities, building conservation groups and agencies such as English Heritage seek to address. Too often, owners guard their properties against all-comers, apparently preferring to see beautiful buildings fall down rather than enter into conservation partnerships.

Devon has lost countless buildings through demolition, redevelopment, fire and war. The process has not ceased. The greatest threats to our beautiful buildings are not planners or developers but time and neglect.

Sham heritage?

Building restoration throws up an ethical point. Is careful renovation and restoration actually cheating? Should we make it clear where the old ends and the new begins? Are we sometimes guilty of fabricating heritage in the name of aesthetics?

Restoration must be preferable to ruination. The key to successful architectural renovation is function – if an old building can be given a new lease of life then it will survive. The Landmark Trust, which turns old buildings into self-catering holiday accommodation, has mastered this art.

The beautiful buildings of the future

Buildings that are being constructed now will become the beautiful buildings of the future – although our tastes may not be able to recognise it. One movement that will surely yield examples is green architecture. Eco-building, with an eye on energy efficiency and sustainability, is an exciting new development in modern architecture.

The atrium at Paignton Zoo Environmental Park, for example, has a grass roof, designed to lessen the environmental impact of the building and – as it helps to keep the building warm in winter and cool in summer – to reduce energy costs. Compared to us, the Victorians never had to think about safeguarding resources such as raw materials and power.

Today materials that are traditional – but more importantly, renewable – such as cob and straw, are being mixed with new technologies such as solar power and thermal insulation. You can even use old newspaper as a building material.

Technical details

Lee Pengelly used two cameras; a Nikon automatic 35mm and a 5x4 inch MPP large-format view camera, both loaded with slow Fuji transparency films.

The MPP is an old-fashioned press camera manufactured in 1965. It has bellows and a ground-glass focusing screen on which the image appears both back-to-front and upside down. It even has a black cloth to put over your head when you're composing the shot.

To combat the problem of converging lines (when the camera lens makes large buildings look as though they are falling backwards) Lee stands his tripod and himself on the roof of his car – though he does get some strange looks from passers-by.

Good news for Devon's buildings

The good news is that there are people and organisations working to help the beautiful buildings of Devon. The Devon Historic Buildings Trust,

Dartmoor National Park Authority, the Devonshire Association, the County Council and local authorities through their conservation officers are all playing their part. Charities such as the National Trust and the Landmark Trust do much to restore and preserve historic and unusual properties.

Building repairs and restorations are expensive. It is worth noting that the National Lottery – in the form of the Heritage Lottery Fund – and Europe have been good sources of funding for the work.

The listing process puts Devon's buildings into context, recognising those that are of national significance. There are something like 500 000 listed buildings in the country – 3500 of these are in Devon.

While too many beautiful buildings are falling into ruin (in Barnstaple, Pugin's Church of the Immaculate Conception stands derelict, the subject of endless rows over money), others are being saved. Plymouth's art deco Tinside Lido is being renovated and in the future should be the jewel in the crown of the Hoe.

Customs House, Exeter Quay, 1681

This building dates from the time of Exeter's flourishing cloth trade. Warm red brick edged in white gives it a stately presence.

Regeneration plans in Devonport could be good news for Foulston's Ker Street group. Meanwhile, there are new moves afoot to find a use for the Royal William Victualling Yard, which has been in the hands of successive development bodies since 1993.

In Exeter the Customs House and Haven Banks power station are included in plans to rejuvenate the quayside. The challenge is to find suitable uses for these large historic buildings.

Working on this book has increased our awareness of the beautiful buildings of Devon – we hope reading it increases yours. The chances are that this collection includes old favourites, introduces some new gems and shows familiar places in a fresh light. This book is a celebration of Devon's beautiful buildings.

Philip Knowling
April 2003

NORTH DEVON

Gazebo, Rosemoor, Great Torrington

This gazebo was saved from decay and collapse by the Devon Historic Buildings Trust. It was dismantled and moved from the middle of Great Torrington to an ideal location at Rosemoor, the RHS gardens just outside the town. Restored and rebuilt, it is now perfectly at home in this splendid garden setting.

Previous: **Cob and thatch privy, Chulmleigh**

Cob – a mix of clay and straw, used wet – is a truly local building material. This form of earth-building yields thick, undulating, organic walls. With a weatherproof footing and sheltering eaves cob will last for centuries.

Pannier Market, Great Torrington, 1842
*The stuccoed and pedimented front of the market house lends
a classical tone to this attractive town centre.*

Town Hall, Great Torrington, 1861
*A solid Georgian-style building, like the market a focal
point in the centre of the settlement.*

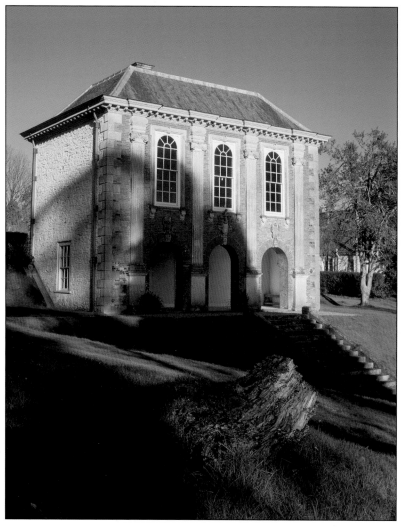

The Library, Stevenstone, Great Torrington
Stevenstone was the principal estate of the Rolle family (who also created Bicton).
The house is now a ruin but this attractive eighteenth-century garden pavilion
is (along with the nearby Orangery) a superb Landmark Trust holiday let.

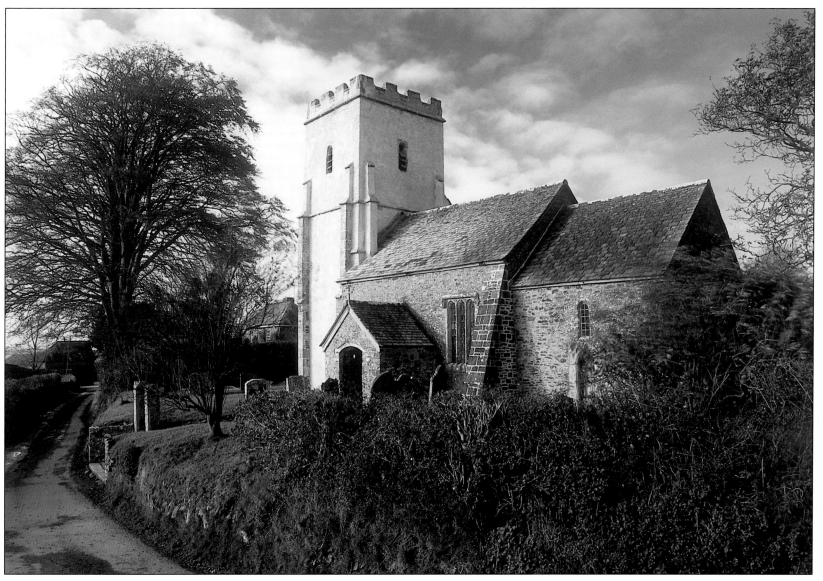

St Mary's Church, Honeychurch, near Sampford Courtenay
A charming little church on the northern fringe of Dartmoor.

Castle Hill, Filleigh, 1730 to 1740

The most impressive country estate in Devon. Castle Hill's long Palladian façade was built for Hugh Fortescue, Lord Clinton (and rebuilt after a fire in 1935). It was designed in consultation with Lord Burlington, one of the most influential men of the eighteenth century.

The grounds were laid out with grand designs reminiscent of Stowe and Stourhead. The Arcadian idyll is dotted with sham castles, triumphal arches, temples and grottoes.

The sixteenth-century Venetian architect Andrea Palladio was inspired by the grand remains of Roman buildings with their pillars, pediments and domes.

Appledore

A village of cottages and larger houses clustered about the estuary of the Taw and the Torridge. Appledore thrived on shipbuilding and trade with North America in the eighteenth and nineteenth centuries, as evidenced by its quays, wharves, warehouses and merchants' houses. The Richmond Yard of 1856 is a dry dock 100 metres (330 feet) long. The shipyard of 1969 is one of the largest covered yards in Europe.

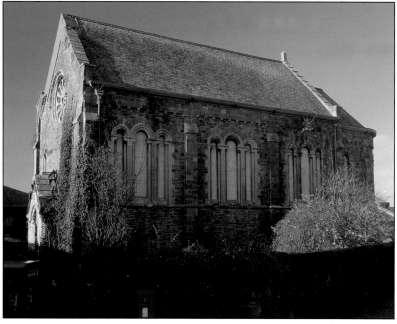

**Church of the Immaculate Conception,
Barnstaple, nineteenth century**

*The design has been attributed to August Pugin, the great Victorian Gothic architect.
Pugin converted to Catholicism and built several Roman Catholic churches. If this is
by Pugin then it is a rare excursion into the Romanesque style, itself an unusual
approach for a Catholic church at that time.*

St Anne's Chapel, Barnstaple

*A chantry chapel probably dating from the early fourteenth century, with a sixteenth-
century tower and Victorian additions. A Grade I listed building.*

Opposite: **Tawstock Court, 1787**

*When the Elizabethan house was largely destroyed by fire in 1787, the country
seat of the Bourchier Wrey family was rebuilt in the Picturesque Gothic style,
with towers, turrets, lancet windows and arches. Now a school.*

Tawstock Tower

A late-eighteenth-century stone folly tower with pointed windows and crenellations – a fantasy playground for children of all ages.
This sham castle lookout has now been sympathetically extended and imaginatively restored to make a wonderful home.

Hartland Point lighthouse, Hartland
The white fortress of the Hartland Point lighthouse stands at the place where the elements of water, earth and air meet with such savage force.

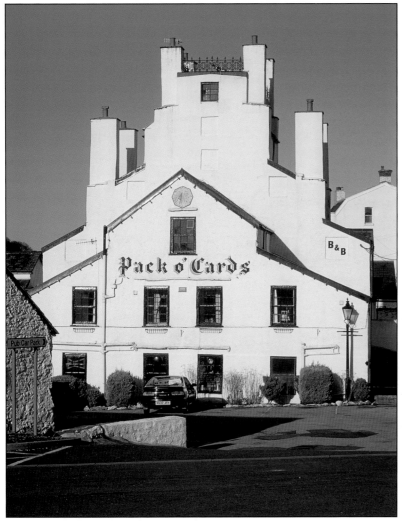

Pack of Cards Inn, Combe Martin, early eighteenth century.
This pub was allegedly built by George Ley to celebrate a famous win at cards, with the number of storeys, rooms, windows and stairways devised to mark the suits and cards of the deck. If you reject the legend you can still appreciate the Venetian windows, Tuscan columns and pilasters on the outside and wood panelling and decorative plaster ceilings inside.

Baggy House, Croyde, twentieth century
A striking modern house in a grand location. Designed by London architect Anthony Hudson, the house is futuristic yet retains shapes and details that echo the Devon vernacular. The building makes the most of its ocean views.

Opposite: **Hartland Abbey**
A secluded medieval abbey that became a country house after the Dissolution of the Monasteries in the sixteenth century. In 1779 the house was given a fantasy Gothic Revival facelift with lancet windows and castellated parapets. In the nineteenth century George Gilbert Scott added some more studious Gothic touches. It's ironic that a building from the original Gothic period should be subject to not one but two later Gothic makeovers.

Landmark Theatre, Ilfracombe
A bold and unusual design – and a shape that is instantly recognised.

Hele Mill, eighteenth century
A fine old corn-mill near Ilfracombe with an overshot water-wheel.

Lee Abbey, nineteenth century
A crenellated, buttressed, pinnacled Gothic wedding cake dramatically sited on the towering North Devon cliffs.

Old Light, Lundy, 1819

A handsome granite form dwarfed by the natural majesty of its setting.
At 27 metres (90 feet) on top of cliffs 170 metres (567 feet) tall, this retired
lighthouse was the highest light in Britain.

St Helena's Church, Lundy, 1896

Built for the wonderfully named Reverend Heaven, the then owner of Lundy.

Clovelly
Famed yet unspoilt, Clovelly is a higgledy-piggledy village of cobbles and cottages clinging to the cliffs, picturesquely frozen in time.

Lynton–Lynmouth incline railway

The cliff railway linking Lynton to Lynmouth opened in 1890, the first and still the longest in England. This part of Devon is famed for its alpine looks and both the railway and the style of its buildings contribute to the atmosphere.

SOUTH DEVON

Dartington Hall, Dartington, fourteenth century
*At the heart of the Dartington estate lies this large medieval courtyard and the superb Great Hall. The estate was revived
in the 1930s under the Elmhirsts as a centre for progressive social thought and educational experimentation.*

Previous: **Bantham boathouse, Aveton Gifford**
A simple building in a magnificent setting.

High Cross House, Dartington, 1931 to 1932, by William Lescaze
*One of the first International Modern houses in England. The stark geometric design blends indoor
and outdoor spaces in a form that is still futuristic today.*

Britannia Royal Naval College, Dartmouth
Every vessel that sails through the mouth of the River Dart is watched over by the long, low, red-brick college buildings.

Mansion House, Dartmouth, 1730

Dartmouth's best eighteenth-century building.

Agincourt House, Dartmouth

Restored, probably dating from the seventeenth century.

Butterwalk, Dartmouth, 1628 to 1640

A wonderful group of timber-framed houses with their upper floors built out over the pavement on granite pillars. Lavishly decorated inside and out, this is conspicuous consumption seventeenth-century style.

Kingswear Castle and Dartmouth Castle

Sailing into the mouth of the Dart is like passing into the jaws of war. The twin fortresses grow out of the sea and the rock and watch over every vessel. A chain could be passed between the castles to close the river to enemy ships.

The Cherub, Dartmouth
*The only complete medieval house in Dartmouth, with
its upper floor jettied out over the street.*

Hill House Nurseries, Landscove, 1851
An old parsonage hung with slate and climbing plants. The gardens and greenhouses are sheltered by tall trees.

Berry Pomeroy castle
A romantic ruin in a splendid setting – a wooded hillside above a steep river valley. The late-medieval castle of the de Pomeroy family had already been abandoned by 1701.

Tower, Slapton
The tower of a fourteenth-century chantry chapel dominates this tiny settlement, hidden inland away from the shingle beach.

Eastgate, Totnes
*This landmark denotes the entrance to the Saxon settlement
and is the point at which Fore Street becomes High Street.
The gatehouse was remodelled in the nineteenth century and
rebuilt after a fire in the twentieth century.*

Bridge Terrace on the Plains, Totnes, by Millwood Homes
A new building with neat Georgian detailing – not a deception but a tasteful blending-in.
It shows what modern designers and developers can achieve.

Totnes Castle
A large Norman motte-and-bailey castle imposed upon the Anglo-Saxon town after the Conquest. It sits like a stone crown on the brow of the hill.

The Old Mill, Wembury
This former mill house, almost on the beach of the Yealm estuary, is now a café.

Burgh Island Hotel, Bigbury-on-Sea, 1930
*Pre-war style in a dramatic coastal setting. There's the added
cachet of being cut off by the tide.*

Opposite: **Flete House, Yealmpton**
*A large, dramatic Victorian mansion set in gardens overlooking
the River Erme. A Tudor mansion was modernised in the
eighteenth and early-nineteenth centuries – some elements
remain. What we see today was created between 1878 and
1885 for Henry Bingham Mildmay, of Baring's Bank.*

Start Point lighthouse
The dramatic location can look tranquil but is always dangerous.

The Old Mill, Bovey Tracey, nineteenth century

*Beside the seventeenth-century bridge over the River Bovey stands a group
of outbuildings around a courtyard with water-wheel and tower. It is
now home to the Devon Guild of Craftsmen.*

Pridhamsleigh dovecote
*A circular structure, with a conical slate roof. Pictured in a sea
of grass and flowers and tinged with lichen, this is
an immensely pleasing little building.*

St Luke's Church, Buckfastleigh, 2002;
Holy Trinity Church, Buckfastleigh

A striking modern design for a small, traditional moorland town.
This church was created by the noted architect, Ron Weeks, who grew
up in Buckfastleigh – it is his thank you to his home town.

The ruins of the former parish church (right), parts of which date from the
thirteenth century, stand on the hill above the town. Holy Trinity was destroyed
by fire in 1992; the new St Luke's was built on the site of a modest
Victorian chapel to replace both it and the medieval church.

Ugbrooke House, 1763 to 1768 by Robert Adam

This house, the seat of the Cliffords since the sixteenth century, was fashionably remodelled in the late eighteenth century. Adam's work here is among his earliest in the castellated style. The grounds, by Repton, are made up of deceptively simple sweeps of grass, trees and water.

Luscombe Castle, 1804, John Nash

Lost in the Haldon Hills is one of the most important buildings in Devon. The house was designed by John Nash, the grounds by Humphrey Repton and the later chapel by Sir George Gilbert Scott. Luscombe was built for the Hoare family, who still own it. A Picturesque fantasy set in its own Arcadian valley.

Rixdale, Dawlish, seventeenth century
A very large farmhouse with accompanying barn. The farm was the seat of the Tripe family.

Limekiln, Starcross

Limekilns are the remnants of a rural industry, when sea shells and limestone were burnt to extract lime for fertiliser and mortar.

Atmospheric railway pumping house, 1845

Designed by Isambard Kingdom Brunel for the South Devon Atmospheric Railway, this is the only surviving atmospheric pump house in the country. In an atmospheric railway the engines (pumping houses) were fixed and the trains were dragged along the track by air pressure in a central pipe. Industrial Italianate in red sandstone, this example is a monument to a technology that was tried and abandoned.

Haldon Belvedere, 1788

One of Devon's best-known landmarks. This elegant white tower rises from the forests of Haldon some 800 feet above sea level and overlooks the city of Exeter. Refurbished in the 1990s by the Devon Historic Buildings Trust, Haldon Belvedere (or Lawrence Castle) is now self-catering holiday accommodation and is licensed for civil weddings.

Opposite: **Powderham Castle**

Between 1845 and 1847 this ancient fortified manor house, home to the Courtenay family, was transformed into a castle. The setting, on the Exe estuary, is glorious.

Forde House, Newton Abbot, seventeenth century
*A much-altered manor house with Dutch gables, tall chimney stacks and a cupola. The extravagant
interiors were created for the visit of King Charles I in 1625.*

Old Forde House is owned by Teignbridge District Council and is available for functions and weddings.

St Luke's Church, Milber, 1936–1963

A stunning design in a Byzantine-Romanesque style with copper pyramidal tower and three converging naves. The vicar was J. Keble Martin, author of British Flora, *the architect was his brother. Keble Martin saw the church in a dream – and built it.*

Newton Abbot Library, 1901 to 1904

Originally the Passmore Edwards Public Library, Science, Art and Technical School. Grey Devon limestone contrasts with yellow ceramic dressings on the front of this flamboyant temple of learning.

Oldway Mansion, Paignton, 1873

Isaac Singer was a colourful character – with wives, mistresses and 24 children, the least interesting
thing about him seems to have been the sewing machine that made his fortune. Oldway was dubbed the
Big Wigwam, but it's a French fantasy made more French by the alterations of Isaac's son Paris.
Between them the Singers built a little Palace of Versailles in Paignton.

Oldway now belongs to Torbay Council and houses – among other things –the local registry office.

Paignton Pier, 1878

Built by Arthur Hyde Dendy, a local entrepreneur who ran a newspaper and owned hotels. He also introduced omnibus services, built a cycle track and was vociferous in his promotion of the town. Nothing evokes the old-fashioned seaside holiday quite like a pier such as this.

Cottages, Cockington, Torquay
Built of stone, cob, thatch and the passage of time, these classic English country cottages are beautifully grouped.
There's barely a straight wall between them…

Cockington Court, Torquay, sixteenth century
An attractive mansion made by its setting in a sweeping green valley.

Cockington Forge, Torquay, late eighteenth century
Built of stone and cob, the thatched roof of this old forge extends out over the open, cobbled work area. It is part of the attractive village of Cockington, hidden away in a lost valley in the midst of the Torbay conurbation.

Hesketh Crescent, Torquay, 1846 to 1848
A crisp, curving terrace of grand houses looking out across the bay.

Redcliffe Hotel, Torquay, 1855 to 1865

The Indian style – 'Hindoo' – is rare in Devon. The Redcliffe was built as a private house for a retired Indian engineer and features elegant Eastern arches, a rotunda and delicate detailing. Its character shines even through the modern extensions.

The Spanish Barn, Torre, Torquay, thirteenth century

The distracting name comes from the brief period in 1588 when Spanish prisoners of war were held here. It is thought to be the oldest surviving barn in Devon. With its buttresses, high porches and long, nave-like interior, this monastic barn is a cathedral to agriculture.

Torre Abbey, Torquay, founded in 1196

The complex of buildings and ruins reflects a long history as religious house, private residence and public space.

Torquay Town Hall, 1906 to 1911, 1935
The main building, with its turrets and domes, is Edwardian baroque. This contrasts with the bold art deco addition of Electric House, built in 1935, a former electricity showroom taken over by the town council and converted into offices.

Torquay Museum, 1874 to 1876
*A Venetian Gothic temple of learning, with terracotta panels over two of the five front windows representing botany
and natural history (the other three are plain because the money ran out).*

EAST DEVON

The Palm House, Bicton, nineteenth century
This is a relatively small but splendidly formed hothouse. The construction – sweeping curves of glass on a slender
iron frame – is testament to the technology of the age.

Previous: **Shute Gatehouse, Axminster**
This grand gateway to Shute Barton is a sham. A sixteenth-century core was romantically extended in the nineteenth century.
Whatever its origins, today Shute makes a wonderful holiday let, courtesy of the Landmark Trust.

The Hermitage, Bicton, 1839
Hidden away in a far corner of the gardens stands the Hermitage, a sweet little wooden chalet with shingled roof, rustic furniture and deer-bone floor. Not in the best of repair, but nonetheless appealing.

St Winfred's Church, Branscombe, thirteenth century

This atmospheric parish church is a rare dedication to an obscure saint. Once under the auspices of Exeter Cathedral,
St Winfred's evolved over the centuries and accumulated a wealth of decoration in wood and stone.

Broadclyst windmill
This mill operated only between 1786 and 1815, but its silhouette still dominates the evening skyline.

Silverton stables, 1839 to 1845

A classical palace of brick, an Italianate villa set down in east Devon. And to think – this was just the stable block of a monumental stately home to be finished in a patent metallic render… The stables are in ruins now but owned by the Landmark Trust, who plan renovation and repair.

Fairlynch, Budleigh Salterton, early nineteenth century

The cottage ornée was part of the Picturesque movement of the late eighteenth and early nineteenth centuries. The fad for whimsical rustic villas led to the building of delightful gingerbread houses for the gentry.

St Andrew's Church, Colyton

Famous for its hexagonal lantern, everyone from the Normans onwards has helped
shape this church. The cockerel weather-vane is the size of a donkey.

The Barn Hotel, Exmouth, 1896
An Arts & Crafts villa with overhanging eaves, large chimneys and pillared veranda. Formerly thatched.

Copper Castle, Honiton
Enough toll houses remain for them not to be a surprise – unless they are painted pink and crenellated.

Cadhay Manor, Fairmile, sixteenth to seventeenth century

This attractive small manor house is built on a courtyard plan. The central space is uniquely decorated in a chequer-board pattern of sandstone and flint.

St Mary's Church, Ottery St Mary
*Historically one of the most important churches in Devon after
Exeter Cathedral. Parts of this large church may date from
the thirteenth century but most of it is fourteenth century.*

Cottages ornée, Sidmouth

The resorts of the east Devon coast are rich in Picturesque-style holiday villas decorated with exuberant fairy-tale features.

Royal Glen Hotel, Sidmouth, eighteenth century

Towards the end of the eighteenth century a farmstead in a wooded valley near the sea was turned into a fashionable cottage ornée.
In 1819 the Duke and Duchess of Kent leased the villa after the birth of the future Queen Victoria. The Duke died there of pneumonia
and his body lay in state. Today this attractive Picturesque villa is the Royal Glen Hotel.

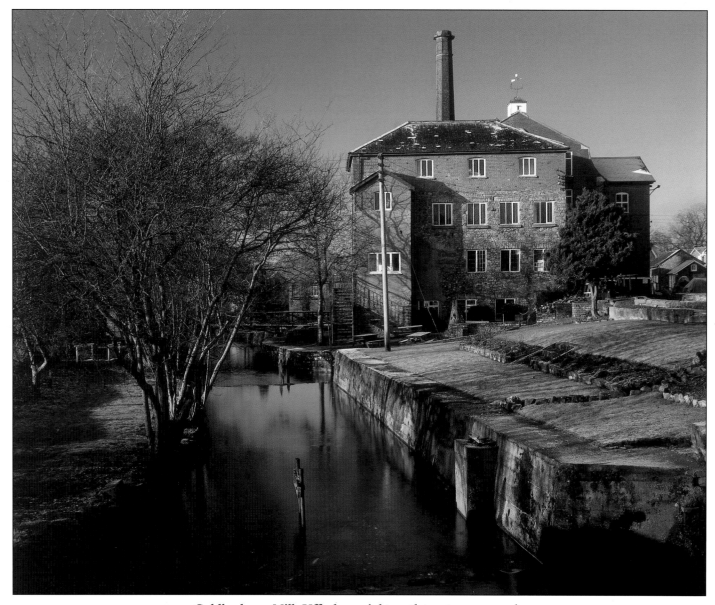

Coldharbour Mill, Uffculme, eighteenth century onwards
A large, stately woollen mill with working waterwheel and steam engine.

AA Call Box, Woodbury Common
Modern traffic speeds by this relic from a slower and more genteel age of motoring.

Hayes Barton, Woodbury
A substantial cob farmhouse built on an E-shaped plan.
The birthplace of Sir Walter Raleigh.

Warehouses, Exeter Quay
These large buildings are symbols of the city's long history as a trading port.

City walls, Exeter

Much of the circuit – originally Roman – survives, though the city has long since outgrown its defensive belt.

Rougemont Castle, Exeter, eleventh century

Built after William the Conqueror took Exeter in 1068. The formidable Norman gate tower now stands in the modern city centre.

Haven Banks electricity generating station, Exeter, 1903
This is a world away from the modern idea of the power station. Built in a time when even industrial buildings were stylish.

Opposite: **Exeter Cathedral, twelfth century onwards**
With its fourteenth-century west front and twin towers, this is one of the most familiar landmarks in Devon. The Cathedral has been at the heart of the city for nearly a thousand years, growing, changing, thriving and surviving.

Cathedral Close

Exeter Cathedral sits in a lawn bordered by houses and shops where medieval mixes with Georgian.
The open space is a place to meet, rest, eat and relax in the centre of the city.

Exeter Guildhall, 1595
*On a busy city shopping street the ancient Guildhall
still claims our attention with its grand entrance straddling
the pavement on broad pillars.*

Royal Albert Memorial Museum, Exeter, 1866
Gothic splendour, a Victorian cathedral of science and learning.

Southernhay West, Exeter, 1789
Graceful and gracious Georgian terracing – well-proportioned and elegant.

St Nicholas Priory, Exeter, eleventh century
The remains of a small Benedictine priory, tucked away off Fore Street.

The House That Moved, West Street, Exeter
*A medieval building famously moved in its entirety
from Edmund Street in 1961.*

Washington Singer Labs, Exeter University Campus, 1931
Named after Washington Merritt Grant Singer (1866–1934), the second son of the second marriage of sewing-machine magnate Isaac Singer, who gave a quarter of the cost of building them. This was the first of five buildings on campus designed by architect E. Vincent Harris.

Colleton Crescent, Exeter, 1814
An elegant late-Georgian terrace with delicate ornamental wrought-iron balconies.

Wynard's Hospital, Magdalen Street, 1435 onwards
Former almshouses, founded in the fifteenth century and altered in the seventeenth, eighteenth and nineteenth centuries.

Imperial Hotel

*A late-Georgian house turned into an hotel. Remarkable for the great, curving form of its airy conservatory,
which came from elsewhere and was added on, to spectacular effect.*

Jaguar car showrooms, Matford, Exeter
The large circular form gives this new building something of a 1930s feel – harking back to the golden age of motoring.

Bickleigh Castle

A fortified manor house in an idyllic setting in the heart of Devon. A complex of buildings dating back at least to the fifteenth century, including a gatehouse, stables and courtyard, as well as a rare twelfth-century private chapel. The Courtenays, the Carews, the Civil War and the twentieth century have all helped make Bickleigh what it is today.

Fisherman's Cott Inn, Bickleigh

*A long, low building beside the River Exe. This spot was the inspiration for one of the most famous songs ever
written – 'Bridge Over Troubled Water' by Paul Simon.*

Holy Cross Church, Crediton

Crediton was the birthplace of Saint Boniface and the seat of a bishop between 909 and 1050. The importance of the town is reflected in its large red sandstone church – 67 metres (220 feet) in length. The church is mostly from the fifteenth century – the oldest parts are twelfth century.

Cob bus shelter, 1978, Down St Mary, Crediton

It's good to see traditional materials being used today. There has been a resurgence in cob building in recent years.

Great Gutton farmhouse, Crediton

A large, late-sixteenth-century farmhouse built in parts of stone, cob, thatch, oak and brick. The small, late-medieval cob-and-thatch barn may have been repaired with corrugated iron and breeze-blocks, but the hayloft, cart-loading bays and cruck trusses are still apparent. This is a farm that has seen many changes, both in its own fabric and in the surrounding landscape.

Old fire station, Tiverton, nineteenth century

*The old fire station and the former police headquarters and borough gaol were restored and converted between 1977 and 1979
by the Devon Historic Buildings Trust. The fire station was built next to the police station because when Tiverton had its own police
force the Chief Constable was also responsible for the fire brigade.*

Old Blundell's, Tiverton, 1604

When it was founded by the bequest of a successful local merchant early in the seventeenth century, this was one of the largest grammar schools in the country. Parts of the old school have been converted into flats.

Phoenix Lane car park, Tiverton, 1990

This is a multi-storey car park that looks nothing like most of its type. Built in 1990 and designed by Bruges Tozer of Bristol, the red brick and mock windows are a world away from the dreary concrete slabs of many car parks. The turrets give the building the feel of an Eastern fortress.

WEST DEVON

Endsleigh House, Milton Abbot, 1810, by Sir Jeffery Wyatville
A cottage ornée for the 6th Duke of Bedford, built during the Picturesque period of the late-eighteenth and early-nineteenth centuries.
Endsleigh has magnificent views of the Tamar Valley and gardens landscaped by Humphrey Repton.

Previous: **The Garden House, Buckland Monachorum**
The house is the former vicarage, built in the nineteenth century to replace its medieval predecessor, the ruins of which stand in the grounds. Seas of flowers and foliage lap around the house itself, the ruins and the other garden structures.

The Swiss Cottage at Endsleigh
The Swiss Cottage stands in the part-natural, part-manipulated landscape of Endsleigh. Deep eaves, ornate rustic woodwork and a large veranda giving onto alpine views make it an imaginative masterpiece. Thanks to the Landmark Trust you can stay here and revel in the atmosphere.

The Dairy at Endsleigh, near Milton Abbot, *c.*1814, probably by Sir Jeffery Wyatville
Two properties – Dairy Dell Cottage and Pond Cottage – form a long, low range with a rustic loggia and small, leaded windows. They sit in Dairy Dell, a secret, miniature landscape of still water and trickling streams created by Repton.

Kelly College, Tavistock, nineteenth century
*A public school in the grand Victorian manner. A complex of buttressed halls, Gothic gables and mock-Tudor wings in local
Hurdwick stone with limestone trimmings.*

Wheal Betsy, 1867
The classic tin-mine outline rises from the moorland like a memorial to a lost industry.

The church of St Michael de Rupe, Brent Tor
*St Michael on the Rock is the highest church in England. It's a dramatic situation – this tiny church, raised up on
a knuckle of volcanic rock, is visible for miles around.*

Toll House, Tavistock
A small, charming, well-sited little toll house.

Belmont House, Plymouth, 1825, John Foulston
*A large, detached villa by the architect who brought the neoclassical
style to Plymouth, John Foulston. This is perhaps his best
surviving villa – nowadays a youth hostel.*

The Royal William Victualling Yard, Devonport, 1827 to 1833, Sir John Rennie Junior

Sir John Rennie finished the breakwater across the Sound and designed the King William complex – and so built his name into the naval heritage of Plymouth. The Royal William Victualling Yard was designed to manufacture, store and distribute all the supplies needed to keep the navy going, from food to gunpowder. Built of limestone and granite, it is a grand and simple monument to maritime power.

Odd Fellows Hall, 1823, John Foulston
*Part of John Foulston's grand grouping of public buildings for Devonport –
an institution in the Egyptian style, beautifully-detailed and evocative.*

Town Hall, Ker Street, Devonport, 1821, John Foulston
*Foulston's grand neoclassical town hall now stands forlorn and
decaying in a far corner of the city.*

Charles Church, Plymouth, 1658
This was one of very few established churches built during the Commonwealth of 1649 to 1660.
Bombed during the Blitz, the roofless ruin now stands as a monument to the devastatation of war.

Crownhill Fort, 1863 to 1872

An outstanding later example of a Royal Commission fort. Built to defend Plymouth and the dockyards from a landward attack, the muscular design of ramparts and gun emplacements is set down defensively into the earth with commanding views over the city.

**The Elizabethan House, Plymouth,
seventeenth century**
*Arguably the most complete and unaltered example of a jettied
merchant's house in Plymouth.*

Fish Market, Plymouth, 1896
Built on reclaimed land by the Sutton Harbour Improvement Company. The cast-iron columns, decorative bargeboards and fretted canopy give it a railway-station style – and indeed the architect was Sir James Inglis, engineer to GWR. It now has a new lease of life as a visitor attraction.

**Merchant's House, Plymouth,
fifteenth century onwards**
*A time-capsule of changing building styles and materials,
restored during the twentieth century.*

National Marine Aquarium, Plymouth, twentieth century
The sweeping shape is clad in wooden planks like the sea-bleached decking of a sailing ship. It is home to the deepest tank in Europe.

The Royal Bank of Scotland, St Andrew's Cross, Plymouth, *c*.1960

This commanding building stands at the end of Royal Parade where post-war Plymouth meets the ancient Barbican district. Originally the National Westminster bank, this is a sort of post-war neoclassical art deco with a grand four-storey portico and a roof-top clock.

**The Bank public house,
Derry's Cross, Plymouth, 1889**

*This former bank is a ghost of the old Plymouth city centre,
with its very different street-plan. A Victorian galleon of a
building, sailing on a sea of concrete.*

Prysten House, Plymouth, *c.*1498
*An excellent large, late medieval merchant's house
with a typical courtyard plan.*

The Royal Citadel, Plymouth, 1665 to 1671
Built on the site of earlier forts, the Citadel has evolved with the art of war; defences, guns and personnel have changed over the centuries.
The lavish baroque gate of 1670 is decorated with trophies and swags.

Smeaton's Tower, 1759, rebuilt on the Hoe, Plymouth, 1882
The famous lighthouse that came back from the sea to a well-earned retirement on the Hoe, from where it keeps watch over the Sound.

The Crescent, Plymouth, by George Wightwick, 1860s
Part of the grand neoclassical scheme of John Foulston and his pupil, George Wightwick. A graceful sweep of restrained elegance in sugar-white stucco.

The *Western Morning News* building, Derriford, Plymouth
The home of this regional daily paper is a ship of glass and steel and light, sailing across the industrial skyline of the city.

Sainsbury's supermarket, Marsh Mills, Plymouth
An otherwise ordinary building is marked out by its amazing canopy, reminiscent of the sails of Arab dhows on the Nile.

Stamford Fort, Plymstock, 1865

*Part of the great ring of Victorian forts built to defend Plymouth and
its naval base from attack by both land and sea.*

Hemerdon House, Sparkwell

Built at the turn of the nineteenth century for James Woollcombe.

DARTMOOR

Slate hanging, Ashburton
Slate has long been used both for building and roofing. In towns such as Ashburton and Totnes it is also hung on the walls for added protection against the weather. In some cases it has been decoratively shaped.

Previous: **Cottages, Buckland–in–the–Moor**
A chocolate-box range of thatch-and-granite cottages nestling in a sheltered fold of the bleak moor.

Lower Jurston, Chagford, fifteenth century onwards
A handsome, sturdy Dartmoor farm.

Bleak House
The name says it all…

Opposite: **Nun's Cross Farm, Dartmoor**
South of Princetown stand the remains of the last smallholding to be taken from the moor.
The foundations are of a farmhouse built in 1870; an abandoned later farm stands nearby.

Lydford Castle

*Lydford is a village that was once an important town,
probably because of its defendable location. Lydford has two
castles – the foundations of an early-Norman fortification lie to
the west of the church. The impressive thirteenth-century ruins
are themselves built on top of twelfth-century remains now
buried by the defensive mound.*

The Warren House Inn, Dartmoor
*Britain's highest pub, the Warren House boasts few locals,
plenty of passing trade and the most magnificent setting in
which to drink a pint of beer.*

Powder Mills, near Two Bridges, nineteenth century
Gunpowder was once made here in this lonely, barren spot. A dangerous job in a distant place.

Clapper bridge, Postbridge

Possibly thirteenth century – but people were crossing the watercourses of Dartmoor many centuries before then.
Clapper bridges are simple, solid and ageless.

Almshouses, Moretonhampstead, 1637

These four almshouses (now two cottages) may incorporate some stone from a medieval hospital. The unusual arcade or loggia has made the building one of the most recognisable on Dartmoor.

Dartmoor Prison
A bleak symbol of justice, as uncompromising as the surrounding moorland.

Saint Pancras church, Widecombe-in-the-Moor, fifteenth century
The 'cathedral of the moor', a granite landmark in a granite landscape.

Grimspound, Hamel Down, near Widecombe
This ancient enclosure filled with hut circles is one of Dartmoor's most famous prehistoric sites.

Sanders, Lettaford, Widecombe-in-the-Moor
A classic Dartmoor longhouse, now owned and preserved by the Landmark Trust.

Old tinners' huts, Burrator; ruined building (opposite)**, Burrator**

The hard life of the moorland tin-worker is commemorated by these ruins (above), made attractive by the slow hands of time and decay.

Bearslake, Sourton, early sixteenth century
A Dartmoor longhouse hunched against the windswept edge of the moor. Despite changes inside, Bearslake retains its attractive exterior.

Okehampton Castle, twelfth century onwards
*These picturesque ruins rise from wooded slopes above the rushing West Okement river. With its Norman motte-and-bailey core
and a range of later additions, it is one of the biggest castles in Devon.*

BIBLIOGRAPHY

Beacham, Peter (editor), *Devon Buildings*, Devon Books, 1990

Born, Anne, *The Torbay Towns*, Phillimore, 1989

Creeke, Julia, *Life and Times in Sidmouth*, Sid Vale Association, 1992

Curl, James, *English Architecture, an Illustrated Glossary*, David & Charles, 1977

Gray, Todd, *The Garden History of Devon*, University of Exeter Press, 1995

Hardy, Paul, *Exeter – Profile of a City*, Redcliffe, 1982

Headley, Gwyn & Meulenkamp, Wim, *Follies, a National Trust Guide*, Jonathan Cape, 1986

Headley, Gwyn & Meulenkamp, Wim, *Follies, Grottoes & Garden Buildings*, Aurum, 1999

Hoskins, W.G., *Devon*, David & Charles, 1978 edition

Landmark Handbook, the Landmark Trust, various

Minchinton, Walter, *Windmills of Devon*, University of Exeter and Exeter Industrial Archaeology Group, 1977

Pevsner, Nikolaus & Cherry, Bridget, *The Buildings of England – Devon*, Penguin, 1989

Pugsley, Steven, *Devon Gardens – an Historical Survey*, Alan Sutton Publishing/Devon Gardens Trust, 1994

Richardson, A.E. & Lovett Gill, C., *Regional Architecture of the West of England*, Halsgrove, 1924, facsimile edition 2001

Stuart, Elisabeth, *Devon Curiosities*, Dovecote Press, 1989

Thomas, Peter, *Images of Devon*, Westcountry Books, 1995

Toyne, Shan, *Devon Privies*, Countryside Books, 1998

CONTACT DETAILS

The Devonshire Association – buildings section
Bowhill, Exeter EX4 1LQ

The Devon Historic Buildings Trust
Mrs Michaela Savage, secretary
20 Shortwood Close, Budleigh Salterton, Devon EX9 6QW
Telephone: 01392 833846

Endsleigh House
Milton Abbot, Devon PL19 0PQ
Telephone: 01822 870248

English Heritage
English Heritage – Customer Services
PO box 569, Swindon SN2 2YP
Telephone: 0870 333 1181
E-mail: customers@english-heritage.org.uk
Website: www.english-heritage.org.uk

Flete House
Ivybridge, Devon
Telephone: 01752 830308

The Garden House
Buckland Monachorum, Yelverton, Devon PL20 7LQ
Telephone: 01822 854769

High Cross House, Dartington
Dartington Hall, Totnes, Devon TQ9 6ED
Telephone: 01803 864114

Landmark Trust
Shottesbrooke, Maidenhead, Berkshire SL6 2SW
Telephone: 01628 825925
Website: www.landmarktrust.co.uk

Tawstock Court
St Michael's, Tawstock Court, Barnstaple, Devon EX31 3HY